Cords and Life's Harmony

Cords that Bind us Together

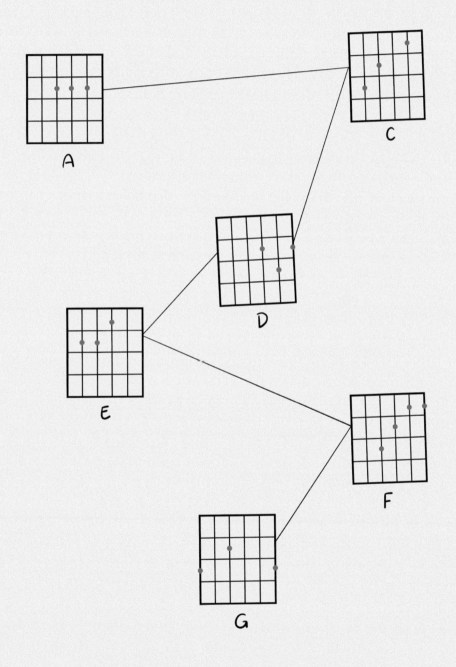

ROBERT ROGERS

To order additional copies of this book, contact:
Xlibris
844-714-8691
www.Xlibris.com
Orders@Xlibris.com

ISBN: Softcover   978-1-6698-1775-8
        EBook   978-1-6698-1776-5

Print information available on the last page

Rev. date: 04/29/2022

Prologue

When playing a musical instrument or singing, your thoughts are concentrated with what you are doing. It blocks troubling thoughts. It's healthy, entertaining, and self-enjoyable.

If you have ever wanted to play the guitar, now is the time **It's easy. Your age doesn't matter**. You don't have to read music or be an accomplished singer. Just dig-out that old guitar and begin forming the cords with your fingers.

A lot of songs can be played only using three, four, or five cords. You can strum the guitar or pick the stings. The cords remain the same.

You and others around you will enjoy how you play and sing.

Contents

Names & Numbers 1

Guitar Tuner 2

Fingering 3

Strumming 4

Open Cords 5

Picking 6

Change 9

Good Times 11

I Don't want to Go Back 13

I Found You 15

It's Just a Guess 17

Listen to Others 19

My Hero 21

Only Heaven Knows 23

Post Office 25

Remembrances 27

Women are Different 29

You Lied to Me 31

Names & Numbers

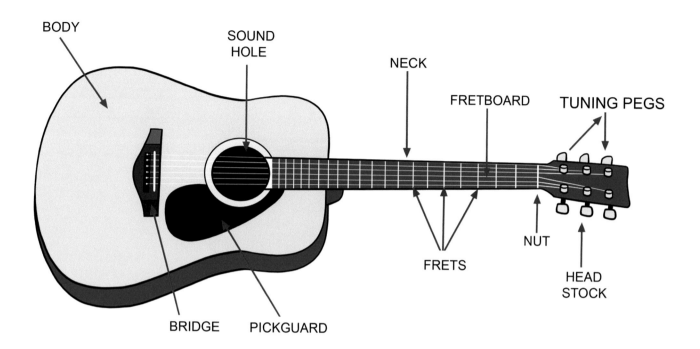

BODY

SOUND HOLE

NECK

FRETBOARD

TUNING PEGS

NUT

FRETS

HEAD STOCK

BRIDGE   PICKGUARD

Guitar String Numbers

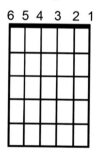

6 5 4 3 2 1

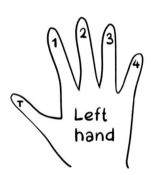

Left hand

Guitar String Names

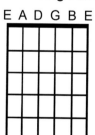

E A D G B E

Guitar Tuner

One of the easiest and accurate tuning methods is to use a small handheld battery powered tuner. They are inexpensive and readily available online or any music store that sells guitars.

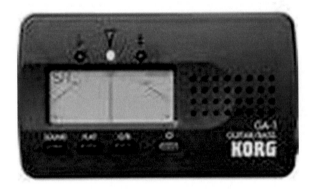

Most small tuners show the string number, and you can adjust each string until the green light is the only one that remains on.

Fingering

Practice a bit each day. Take 5 to 20 minutes fingering the cords and strumming the strings. The fingers you place on the strings may initially be a bit tender but in a while, perhaps a month, that tenderness will disappear. On an acoustic guitar with nylon strings, rather than steel strings, fingers will be a bit more comfortable. **Don't give up**. It's your desire to play that improves your playing ability.

Place the tip of your finger on the strings and press straight down.

Nylon Strings

Steel Strings

Strumming

There are many ways to strum the strings. Here are two easy methods.

1. Finger a cord and strum down all the strings with your thumb. You can also strum down and then strum up. Try this pattern:

   Down   Down   Down   Up
   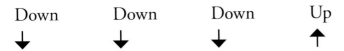

2. Thumb stroke (pluck) the guitar string directly above where you place the top finger on a cord, pause a moment, then with the thumb strum all the strings below. You may want to strum the bottom strings only once or perhaps more.

You can develop more advanced strumming and picking as you seek more variety and different sounds.

Strum the strings as slowly or as fast as you please. **Do what you like and sounds best**

Enjoy your improving ability and the sounds.

Note: When playing the G cord, thumb stroke the top #6 (E) string

Open Cords

The most commonly used cords are called "open" cords because they contain at least one open (not fretted) string. The cords are most often used with the first four frets. With the help of a capo, you can play even a greater range of sounds. The capo shortens the playable length of the strings providing a higher pitch.

The " X " indicated the strings are not played.

Major Cords

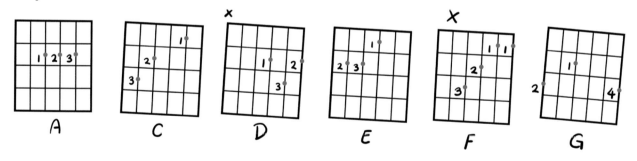

Minor Cords

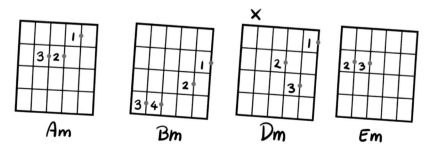

Picking

Here are a couple of basic picking techniques:

Finger the cords like you do when strumming the guitar.

Thumb stroke the guitar string directly above where you placed the top finger on a cord. Pause a second and then with fingers 1,2,3 simultaneously pick the bottom three strings—G,B,E. Finger 4 (the little finger) is not used to pick the strings.

Try this: Pick the bottom three strings three times before stroking with the thumb.

A variation is to use the same process except instead of simultaneously picking the bottom three strings, pick each bottom string separately starting with finger 3 picking string 3 (G). Then pick string 2 and then string 1.

Note: You don't need to have long fingernails. The tips of the fingers work well.

G

D

Em

Change

G
I hope she knows

I loved her so

My life has moved at a rapid pace
         D
l look at my life and wonder

What would I change
      G
A lot of things

I wouldn't drink that much

Neglect a woman's touch
Em
Show a little class
       D
Made love last
G
I should have smiled and kissed her
D
Held her tight

Made things right
G   D
I no longer know how to rhyme
G
I should change the words
          D
I've made lot of mistakes
            Em
My life shall soon be surrender

I hope she remembers

                    Em
I wonder how she will feel
G   D
I hope she knows I loved her so

A

D

G

E

Good Times

A   D
What happened to the good times?
G
It's a nostalgic song

Sung in the past
            A
And will not last

I listened to that music

And remember how it moved me

I understood the words
        G
That's different

I drove the cars that were real machines

I shifted the gears
            D
That's no longer needed
Em
Kids don't remember
G
We danced to rock and role

Listened to Peter Paul and Mary

And Elvis
Em
What happened to the good times?

A thumb would get you a ride
            E
People cared

The world was safe
A   D
What happened to the good times?

A quarter could call someone you loved

A mobile phone has taken its place
           G
We all have one

The phone booth has disappeared

I remember the drive-in movie
           D
The girl at my side

The kiss she would provide
A   G
What happened to the good times?

Em

D

G

I Don't want to Go Back

We dream of yesterday
Many say yesterday was the best of times
We now walk in a different light
Was yesterday the best of times?

Em
We have forgotten what life was like
G
I don't want to go back

I picked cotton beside my mother
            D
Watched her cry
                    Em
Stayed hungry all the time

It was a darker time
D
Yesterday wasn't the best of times
                    Em
It only lives in our minds
G
Today's world is a different place

We walk at a different pace

I don't want to go back

I walked to the one-room school in the
            D
deep snow
G
Cut wood so mother would know
                        D
Shifted gears in that rusty old Ford
                        G
Got drafted and lived through a war

I don't want to go back

Television was not there

Outer space was just talk
                                    D
Today we live in a much brighter place
Em
We still have our troubles
D
But I don't want to go back
G
Yesterday wasn't the best of times
                        D
I enjoy walking in today's sunshine

G

D

Em

A

I Found You

I found you
G
Let me walk with you

This sidewalk leads to an ending place
                                       D
Let us walk to a loving place

I have always loved you
G
Please forget what I have done

I do love you so

Hold my hand
           D
Don't let go

Let us walk together
                      Em
I know I've done wrong
         D
Forgive me

We have drifted apart
               A
It was my fault

Help me
D   G
Let us recover our love

Walk with me
Em
Time has changed me
                            G
I know how you feel

I regret what I have done

Let us recover our love
G
I will never again do you wrong
                      Em
Let us rekindle our love

Please trust me

I now know what lasting love can be

Tightly hold my hand

Save me

A

D

It's Just a Guess

A
Men seem to like me

I'm not sure what they see

I don't search for them they come to me

As I walk along the sidewalk
                                 D
They smile and walk beside me

We talk and they want to hold my hand

I smile and tell them no

How far should I go

Should I tell them so

They mean no harm

They just like me

I willingly walk with them

Maybe I should change this dress

It's just a guess

I may let one hold my hand

Fulfill my guess
A
Men just seem to like me

A

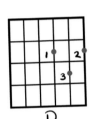

D

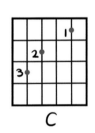

C

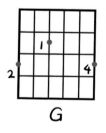

G

Listen to Others

A
Sit by my side

Listen to what I say
                    D
You will remember it someday

When I was as young as you

I thought I knew just what to do
            C
I was wrong

Life moves in different ways

I wanted to change the world
                            D
Make it turn for the love of man
Em
I can't change the world
G
We all move in different ways

You must listen to others
                    C
Learn what they know

Remember I told you so

Our intentions are like sand
                                G
It shifts through our minds and hands

Remember others have different dreams
Em
Just listen

My Hero

A
He is my hero

I love him so
D
He doesn't seem to know

I have often told him so

He just smiles
A
I want him to know he is my hero
D
When we are near my heart beats faster

I love him so

He saved me from my mistakes
A
Held me tight

Told me it's alright

I sometimes cry

When will he ever know
Em
I love him so
G
Hero's never reveal how they feel
D
Holds my hand a tells me not to cry

I somehow believe him

I will stay beside him

Smile

Love is not alone

It lives in us all

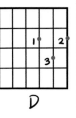

Only Heaven Knows

A
Our lives can't be predicted

Life moves at its own pace
                            Em
This is a strange world

Only heaven knows

Clouds remain
              G
Rain comes and goes

We don't know what life will bring
                        D
It renders hate, love, rain, and snow

We don't know

I know you still love me

Kiss me again
                G
Let's do what we once did

Walk from this house

Go to that old hotel

Do what we once did

Make our love last

Let's do what we once did

Take off our clothes

Touch each other
        D
Feel the warmth

See the sparkle in our eyes
E
Laugh

We will love each other for a long, long time

Post Office

C
I met her at the Post Office

She turned and looked at me

A smile crossed her lips
A
I was fascinated

What could this be

I moved closer

She pressed against me
C
I think she liked me

I just waited to see
Em
Her package fell
D
And so did I

She was as pretty as could be

She smiled at me

I asked would you like some company

She looked with glowing eyes
Em
And said I might

We moved closer

I felt her warmth

She did not decline
A
The Post Office?

Why not?

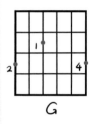

G

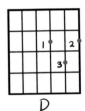

D

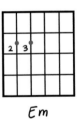

Em

Remembrances

When I was young it was a time to play
Now I don't feel that way
It's the fast-moving years

G
When I was 18 I drove that Ford

Met a girl

We laughed and held hands
        D
Life was fun

I cruised down the night lights
G
Kissed that girl with the red hair

And watched her smile

We were young
           Em
We now walk slow

We gently comb our grey hair

We feel the passing years
G
I remember that red hair

We can't return there
Em
We live in changing years

Women are Different

G
He said

My boy you lack the experience of a man

I will explain what I can

When older you will know what I mean

Let me tell you something about girls and women
A
Don't look at me that way

Listen to what I say

Women know about life

Now listen to your Grandad
A
You may think battles only include men

Women suffer the same

They live through the pain

Struggle to find what can be gained
G
You may find a woman to share your love someday

Tell her how you feel

Hold her close
A
Now don't look away

Listen to what I say

It will help you someday
G
Women are different

You Lied to Me

G
You lied to me
              D
You said you loved me
Em   D
I cannot mend this heart
G   Em
I don't know where to start

I feel guilty

Tears run down my face

It's hard to let go
G
I did love you so

You didn't love me
D
You closed the door
Em
Never open it again
                D
My tears will not fade
G
I will always remember
            D
You closed the door
Em
I did so love you
G
I tried

You said you loved me

You lied

You wanted more
Em
I tried

You said things were right

You lied
                G
I should have known

Searched for the truth
Em
Love Is uncertain
G   Em
It lives in an unknown place
G
Can you walk away
                Em
Start a new life
        D
I wonder
G
Lies last forever

Printed in the United States
by Baker & Taylor Publisher Services